Only Child—Clues for Coping

Only Child—Clues for Coping

Charlotte Foltz Jones

The Westminster Press
Philadelphia

Copyright © 1984 Charlotte Foltz Jones

All rights reserved—no part of this book may be reproduced in any form without permission in writing from the publisher, except by a reviewer who wishes to quote brief passages in connection with a review in magazine or newspaper.

Book design by Christine Schueler

First edition

Published by The Westminster Press®
Philadelphia, Pennsylvania

PRINTED IN THE UNITED STATES OF AMERICA
9 8 7 6 5 4 3 2 1

Library of Congress Cataloging in Publication Data

Jones, Charlotte Foltz.
   Only child—clues for coping.

   Includes index.
   SUMMARY: Advice for the only child on being lonely, being spoiled, taming one's feelings, having friends, and the advantages and disadvantages of being a child with no siblings.
   1. Only child—Juvenile literature. 2. Family—Juvenile literature. [1. Only child. 2. Family life]
I. Title.
HQ777.3.J66 1984   649 '.142   84-10388
ISBN 0-664-32718-4

This book is dedicated to

My son, *John,* who has shown me the joys of being an only child

My husband, *Bill,* whose steadfast belief and encouragement made this book possible

My parents, *Forrest* and *Mildred Foltz,* who taught me love, laughter, and courage

Contents

	Introduction by Susan Rosenzweig	*9*
1.	Who's an Only Child?	11
2.	Why No Sisters or Brothers?	13
3.	Why Some People Have Brothers or Sisters	26
4.	Parents and Other Kinds of Family	30
5.	A Friend Is Someone Who . . .	42
6.	Feelings—How to Tame Them	55
7.	Alone Is Not Lonely	60
8.	It's Not Always Easy	73
9.	Who's Spoiled?	80
10.	As Others See You	86
11.	Minuses in Being an Only	92
12.	Pluses in Being an Only	95
13.	Famous Only Children	101
	Index	*105*
	About the Author	*109*

Introduction

Only children are often considered spoiled, selfish, lonely, overprotected, or maladjusted. This myth began almost one hundred years ago when a psychologist looked at a few teachers' reports on single children. Fortunately, later research showed that, in fact, only children are socially outgoing, independent, self-confident, and cooperative. They tend to be smarter, more creative, and more ambitious than children with siblings.

But the myth persists. The recent favorable research has received much less media attention than the earlier studies. As a result, although being an only child—and having an only child—is becoming much more socially acceptable, the old myths are hard to erase.

Charlotte Foltz Jones, in this book, provides the only child with helpful ideas and sound information. And it is fun to read, too. Here are all the advantages and problems of being an only.

There are many kinds of only children. A person can have a brother or sister and still be considered an only child. With a brother who is fifteen years older and no longer living at home, a youngster is really growing up as an only child. The author gives many other ways of being an only.

Here, also, are good ideas for what an only child can do when feeling bored or lonely or pressured by parents. And here is excellent advice for making and keeping friends and for controlling one's feelings. One chapter tells about onlies who have become famous in many fields.

The information in this book will be useful, too, for friends who have brothers or sisters, for parents, and for teachers and other adults. Everyone needs to learn more about what it is like to be an only child.

SUSAN ROSENZWEIG
*Director of Information
Center for Early Adolescence
University of North Carolina*

1
Who's an Only Child?

There is no doubt for certain people that they are "only children." Each one was the first, last, and only child in the family.

For others, however, it is not quite so simple.

Brian was an only child. That is, he was an only child until his parents got a divorce . . . and his mother married a man with three boys, plus she and Brian's stepfather had a baby girl, after which Brian's father married a woman with two girls, giving Brian three stepbrothers, one half sister, and two stepsisters. To make the family even more complicated, Brian lives with his grandparents.

Is Brian an only child?

Technically, no. But Brian is growing up with no brothers or sisters (of course, all his grandparents' children are adults and not living at home), so actually Brian is being raised as an only child.

Marcia is another typical case: Marcia's only brother is fourteen years older than she. He has not lived at home since Marcia was four years old. Even then, he was so much older that he was almost an adult. So, while technically Marcia is not an only child, she is being raised with no brothers or sisters at home, so she, too, can be considered an only child.

Who is the "only child" this book is written for? Any readers who consider themselves "only children," any who feel as if they are being raised as only children, anyone who is related to or is a friend to an only child.

The situations in this book are those faced by the youngster

- who doesn't have a live-in chess opponent
- who doesn't have someone to blame for putting the peanut butter jar in the refrigerator empty
- who doesn't need to make an appointment to use the bathroom
- who doesn't have someone who screams 83 times a day, "I'm going to tell Mom!"

Growing up as an only child is different from growing up with brothers or sisters. In some ways it is better. In other ways it can be worse.

So if you're an only child, here's how to cope.

2
Why No Sisters or Brothers?

Have you ever wondered, Why am I an only child?

Are you awfully, horribly, incredibly, extremely, very, very ugly? If so, that could be why you are an only child.

Or if you have gorilla breath or tortoise feet or a horrendous appetite for chocolate-covered grasshoppers, that could be another reason.

Maybe you have decided, "Golly, I'm so dumb, my folks were afraid to have another kid for fear it would be just like me."

Of course you know these aren't really the reasons. As someone once said, "All people are beautiful in their own way." Besides, gorilla breath and tortoise feet can be cured. And chocolate-covered grasshoppers can be eaten in a closet with the door closed. And really dumb people can't read books like this.

So why are you an only child?

There are probably many reasons. There are problems parents face that are none of your business (or so they say). There's a chance you might never be told the *real* reason.

It doesn't really matter why you are an only, but lots of people—and maybe you're one—are just naturally curious. They won't stop wondering or asking until they get an answer that satisfies them.

Here are some of the reasons that might explain why you are an only child.

Money

Fifty or sixty years ago a child meant wealth for the family. The child helped in the family business or worked outside the home. The more children a family had, the more work could be done on the farm or the more income could be earned to help the family. Children were a financial asset. This is still true in some cultures.

Today, however, most children do not bring money into the family. Today every child costs.

One day the U.S. Government asked its most reliable computer, "How much does a child cost its parents?"

Knowsalot, as that particular computer was affectionately referred to, replied, "Between $85,000 and $134,000 is how much it will cost to raise a child. And that does not include extras such as baby-sitters or college costs!" (Knowsalot knew nothing about parents' Saturday-night habits and the frequency with which baby-sitters are considered a necessity.)

Knowsalot included necessities such as:

Why No Sisters or Brothers? 15

clothing	electricity	Valentine cards
food	heat and air-	Fourth of July
shelter	conditioning	fireworks
schoolbook fees	hot water	telephone
doctor fees	insurance	automobile
medicine	cage for Her-	car expenses
wart removal cream	man, the hamster	gym suits Sunday shoes
dental services	food for Her-	slippers
birthday presents	man, the hamster	sneakers boots
school play costumes	additional cages for Herman's	jogging shoes basketball
lunch money	children	shoes
fire extin-	Easter baskets	soccer shoes
guishers	Halloween costumes	tennis shoes

Knowsalot probably did not take into consideration:

piano lessons	allowances	prom dresses
voice lessons	magazine sub-	football helmets
tambourine lessons	scriptions summer camp	cheerleading costumes
guitar lessons	camp clothes	roller skates
ballet lessons	skis	roller rink
karate lessons	ski boots	admission
riding lessons	ski poles	ice skates
swimming lessons	ski clothes lift tickets	ice arena admission
swimming suits	a computer	movie money
pool fees	scout uniforms	video games

At last check, none of these things was free.

A couple with a limited income might say, "All this

for one child is expensive. What if we had two children? Twice the expense? Wow!" Then they decide to limit their family to one child in order to give that one child a better quality of life, or at least the necessities.

Noise

Don't laugh.

Anyone who has ever had to listen to two youngsters decide who gets to be the doctor and who has to be the patient knows about noise.

Anyone who has ever had to hear two children decide which TV show to watch knows about noise.

One mother said, "With two children you get *ten* times as much noise—plus all the extra flu viruses."

Time

Some onlies complain about their food, but others complain about their family life, saying, "There just isn't enough time together."

But with brothers or sisters in the family, that time would be even less. Time together would be shared with all the other children.

Some parents have extremely busy schedules. Their time is consumed by work, hobbies, grandparents, canning peaches, balancing their checkbook, jogging, or other obligations. If there is a lot of time pressure, the parents probably feel they can enjoy only one child.

When both mother and father work outside the home, there isn't much time to spend together. If there were more children, the limited time would be divided even further.

Energy

After a long race, you feel tired. You need a rest before you can run again. Probably you would rather do something else than run another race for a while.

This is the way many parents feel. They are tired. They need a rest. And they limit their family to one child because they would rather do something else than deal with another child.

You may find "tired all the time" hard to understand. Most young people are not tired all the time. But "tired after the race" is the way parents may feel every day as they run the race of life.

Priorities

Parents have to set priorities.

Perhaps a clean bathroom is at the bottom of a mother's list of priorities, while leading a pack of Cub Scouts is at the top. Perhaps car maintenance is at the bottom of a father's list of priorities, while his job is near the top. Or vice versa.

An only child can fit nicely on almost any list of priorities. A parent who collects coins can easily take one child to a coin show. But with two or three children, the parent might spend more time disciplining and settling arguments than enjoying the coin show.

Somewhere adults have to draw a line on what they can do and what they might like to do. They are limited by money, time, and physical energy. They have to set priorities—and sometimes that does not include another child.

Marriage Problems, Fights, or Divorce

A couple may have a wonderful wedding. They get along fine the first few weeks together. Then their differences come out. The differences may become more serious and develop into fights. If they have one child, they might fight over:

> Whether to give the baby a bottle
> Whether to let the kindergartner walk to school alone
> Whether to give the child piano lessons and whether to yell when that child doesn't practice
> Whether to let the teenager play football
> Whether to allow three-hour phone conversations

These issues can lead to increased fighting between parents. And the fighting over one child would double with two children. "Who needs it?" some say. And they limit their family to one child.

In a few homes the disagreements are very serious. The parents can see that their marriage might not last. Then they decide: "We already have one child who is going to be hurting when we get a divorce. Why should we bring another child into the world just to suffer from our problems?"

Besides, for a single parent, raising one or two children may be difficult. A single parent raising a batch of children could be a nightmare.

Health

Health reasons sometimes limit a couple to only one child. Occasionally a woman has problems when she gives birth to a baby. Her health might be in danger if she had more children. Her doctor recommends that she stop with one.

Some families have diseases that follow the bloodline. The parents may be advised that it is not a good idea to risk having another child when the chances of a second baby's escaping the disease would be small.

Small children are a lot of work. If a mother or father has health problems, one child may be all they can handle.

Another consideration is that the parent who is earning the family money might not feel able to support more than one child.

Adoption

Adoption might influence how many children are in a family.

Families that adopt a child often have to wait years and years and years for that child. There are very few babies available to be adopted in the United States today. After a couple gets one child, they may not try to get on the list to adopt more children.

Some agencies have a limited supply of children available for adoption. If a family gets one child, they are not allowed any more. So the adopted child is an only child.

Desire for Only One Child

Some parents love their child very much.

But one child is all they want. One child is all it takes to change a husband and wife into parents.

Parents' Careers

Some parents work to get money.

Some parents work to get out of the house.

Some parents work because they love the challenge of their jobs or enjoy the type of work they do.

More than half the women in America have jobs outside the home. More than half the men in America have jobs outside the home. Whatever the reason for working, a job drains the time and energy of a parent, leaving a smaller amount of time and energy to be spread among all the children—or to be given to an only child.

If both parents have a career, someone has to raise the child—or children. That "someone" probably

Why No Sisters or Brothers? 21

charges money. That someone teaches the child—or children—a lot of information and attitudes.

Some parents can't afford to pay more money to someone to take care of more children. Some parents do not like what the first child learned, and so they do not want to chance having a second child taught the same.

If you are old enough so that you don't have a someone, your parents probably feel relieved to be past the baby-sitter hassles. They probably don't want to start over again.

Population Explosion

Many adults are concerned about the future of the planet Earth. They see the increase in the number of people in the world as a serious threat to humans and their food supply. They feel that there are already enough people in the world, and they do not want to add to the overpopulation. Having only one child gives them the opportunity to enjoy parenthood while not overpopulating the planet.

The Unknown

As parents live—and get older—they see problems that other children have. They see children who are sick, children who cause their parents many problems, children who turn out badly no matter how good their homelife was.

Then parents wonder, Could this happen to *our* second child?

They see the money another child would cost, the time it would take, the energy necessary, the way it might affect the entire family—including the children.

This seems to be an even greater problem among older parents. They have the experience to measure time, money, and energy. It might come down to actually fearing the unknown.

History

We all know about Cain and Abel's unhappy relationship as brothers. While most brothers and sisters don't resort to such violence, many people who had bad experiences with their brothers or sisters refuse to put their child through such torture.

> If your parents and their brothers or sisters fought a lot . . .
> If they had to share everything . . .
> If they had no privacy . . .
> If they had to provide free baby-sitting . . .

Some of these experiences might be reasons why you are an only child.

Sometimes a person does not want history to repeat itself. Bad experiences of their own might be the reason your parents limited their family to just one child.

Age

Whether or not to have more children often depends on the parents' ages.

Parents who are twenty-five when they have Baby No. 1 will be forty-seven when that child graduates from college. A second baby when the parents are twenty-eight would make them fifty when No. 2 graduates from college. That still leaves about fifteen working years till retirement for the parents (since most people plan to retire at the age of sixty-five).

But a couple who has Baby No. 1 when they are thirty-four will be fifty-six when Baby No. 1 is out of college. If Baby No. 2 arrives when the parents are thirty-eight, that would mean they are only about five years away from retirement when No. 2 graduates from college.

Some people simply do not want to give so many years to child rearing. Or they realize that the expenses of Baby No. 2 would greatly deplete their retirement savings.

Older parents often get tired quickly. They may feel they have only enough energy to keep up with one child.

In the past, older mothers ran a greater risk of having a child who had a birth defect, according to medical authorities. So mothers over the age of thirty-five may still decide against having another child.

Patience

Some parents can smile and talk softly through their child's temper tantrums, back talk, and general misbehavior. Other parents, however, find out with their first child that their patience is not as great as they had hoped. A second child would only put more pressure on them and more stress on the family.

Work

Babies' diapers have to be changed.

Children need a chauffeur to get to school activities, Scouts, Little League, lessons, and swimming.

Children need parents to volunteer for Scouts, Little League, and party chaperone.

Children need to have their shoes tied.

Children need to have their hot dogs cooked.

Children need to have their teddy bears mended.

Children need to have their socks washed.

Children need to have their parent-teacher conferences scheduled.

Children need to have books read, swings pushed, bedrooms painted, and temperatures taken.

Let's face it: As lovable as you are, you do make some work for your folks. Twice as many children would mean twice as much work. Maybe your folks think enough is enough. Other parents may decide to cope with the problems as they come along, and they invest their love in more children.

Perfection

One parent, when asked why there was only one child in the family, said, "We didn't need to have two kids. We got it right the first time."

Maybe that's why you're an only child!

3
Why Some People Have Brothers or Sisters

When two women meet at a party and begin talking, what is the second question they ask each other? (Question No. 1, of course, is, "Did you see the spots on her glassware?")

The second question is usually, "Do you have children?"

Ask any mother, and she'll probably assure you that no one has ever asked, "Do you have *a* child?" No, it's always plural, more than one: child*ren*.

What "They" Said

Until recently it was thought undesirable to have only one child. Children were a status symbol. A man with seven offspring was seven times as likely to be elected to the school board as the father of only one child.

Over one hundred years ago a man who was supposed to be an expert on children said, "Being an only child is a disease in itself." (A disease? Do you suppose he was working on a vaccine?)

About sixty years ago a husband and wife who were psychologists (Smiley and Margaret Blanton) said, "The only child is greatly handicapped. He [she] cannot be expected to go through life with the same capacity for adjustment that the child reared in the family with other children has."

In other words, these people were saying, children who don't have brothers or sisters won't be able to get along with other people. They won't fit in with friends. They won't get along with teachers. And when they grow up, they won't be able to get along with a husband or wife, a boss, or anyone else.

Parents feared that an only child would grow up to be selfish, spoiled, and unable to live in the give-and-take of the adult world.

Relatives and friends told parents that it was "unfair" to raise the child alone without brothers and sisters.

Although these old stories have been proved untrue, many people still believe them. So some parents have another child just because of what other people say.

Maybe parents should be admired for the bravery it takes to go against what "everyone" else says and to raise an only child!

Luckily, today most people have a broader view of family life. To have only one child is not criticized so much anymore.

In fact, many psychologists have reported working with children who would have been better off in a home with no brothers or sisters. And, once in a while, when children who have too many problems are removed from their parents' homes, they are put in homes where there are no other children.

Some People Will Believe Anything

Some people have a second child because they have been told:

- The second child will be easier to raise because the first child made them "experienced" parents (experienced in hollering, spanking, and cleaning up after an upset stomach)
- The older child will be a teacher (they find out later the older child's teaching was *not* what the parents had in mind!)
- The first child will have a companion (too bad they didn't get the youngster a nice hive of bees instead)
- The older child will serve as a model for the second (and wear out the clothes so the second child wears holey tennis shoes)
- Something is wrong with people who only have one child (but *some* people think there is something wrong with eating mushrooms)
- Housework has to be done anyway, and it's just as easy to clean up after two as one (especially if you have twice as much time and energy to spend cleaning up after both of them)
- The second child will cost less (unless he or she refuses to wear holey tennis shoes)

- Only children are spoiled brats and are selfish, overindulged, maladjusted, uncooperative, temperamental, aggressive, demanding, conceited, domineering, and egotistical.
- Only children are shrinking violets and are unpopular, shy, timid, overdependent, unassertive, and won't stand up for their rights

Television doesn't help matters. Shows like *The Brady Bunch, Eight Is Enough,* and *The Waltons* make raising a large family look easy, fun, and even glamorous. They make living in a family with lots of children seem like a real dream, but they give no suggestions for what a child from a big family should do if he or she doesn't have an appointment to use the bathroom.

Some parents dread their old age. They are afraid they will be all alone. So they figure that with two children there is twice as good a chance that someone will look after them when they get old. Some people have fourteen children so their chances of having someone take care of them when they're old will be fourteen times as good.

So some only children get brothers or sisters.

On the other hand, some parents just plain enjoy children. The more the merrier.

4
Parents and Other Kinds of Family

Anyone with a mean big brother will tell you that life isn't easy.

Anyone with a bratty little sister will tell you that life isn't easy.

Anyone with brothers or sisters of any age will tell you that life isn't easy.

And you can probably tell them a thing or two about how life as an only child isn't easy either.

But luckily, you can tell anyone who is interested that life as an only child can also be great.

Traditional Family

The traditional family for a rabbit is a mother and eight brothers and sisters, with another eight babies soon to join the family.

However, humans are a little different from rabbits.

The traditional family in America is . . . well, it's a mystery.

When your parents were young, a traditional family was a mother, a father, and two offspring. Dad went to work and Mom stayed home and baked cook-

Parents and Other Kinds of Family 31

ies. Grandma almost always lived nearby.

Today over half the women in America have jobs outside the home.

Today there are many one-parent families (one estimate says 16 percent of all families).

Today more people move to other cities or states, and that means fewer children have grandparents or aunts and uncles who live nearby.

So today there is really no "average" or "traditional" family.

Divorced Families

Sometimes, onlies are only children because there was a divorce or possibly a death of one parent before a brother or sister could be added.

An only child and an only parent are still a family. But the relationship may be a little special.

When parents of an only child get a divorce, what happens to the child?

Sarah's parents are divorced. Sarah said, "When my father moved out, things really changed at home. I was only eight years old at the time, but all of a sudden I had a different relationship with my mother. She would ask *me* things like what I thought we should have for supper or whether *I* thought a dress looked okay on her or whether *I* wanted to see a certain movie. In some ways it was fun. I felt important, like what I thought really mattered. But in other ways it was hard. Sometimes I didn't want to be the one to decide. I wasn't always sure of myself enough to feel I could make a decision."

Divorce is hard for anyone, but an only child has to face the problems and adjustments alone.

Brothers and sisters can usually talk about their feelings together, or at least know someone else is hurting the same way. But not always. Some brothers and sisters cannot communicate no matter how much they need one another.

When there's just one, it sometimes seems as if no one cares. Parents are either fighting, crying, worrying about money, meeting with lawyers, making decisions, or "busy with their own problems." The child is probably caught in the middle, and maybe the parents are even taking advantage of the child's place there. Sometimes an only child is tugged in both directions.

Grandparents or aunts and uncles, if they live nearby, may take sides, leaving the child alone in loving both parents.

After the divorce, a child will probably be living with just one parent, and that parent will probably have a job, which means the child will have a lot of time alone. It may seem like forever, but after the divorce is final, child and parent can settle into a routine and life will get easier.

To get life going again after a divorce, join a club or other after-school activity, take lessons in guitar, swimming, karate, sketching, or any special hobby.

Helping others as a volunteer in nursery school, hospital, or retirement home may ease the hurt, too. See page 66–69 for more suggestions.

One advantage in being an only child in a divorce situation is that the time with the other parent (the one who doesn't live in) doesn't have to be divided or shared with brothers and sisters.

A relative, teacher, or counselor can often help in getting through this difficult time.

Some helpful books are:

> *What's Going to Happen to Me? When Parents Separate or Divorce* by Eda LeShan (Four Winds Press, 1978)
>
> *Surviving Your Parents' Divorce* by Charles Broeckman (Franklin Watts, 1980)
>
> *The Boys and Girls Book About Divorce* by Richard A. Gardner (Jason Aronson, 1970)

Death of a Parent

Jason felt almost abandoned when his father died. "I felt so alone," Jason says. "It was like Mom didn't want to talk about Dad. If I said something, she would usually start crying and go to her room and close the door. I just wanted to talk to someone so bad. Mom and I got along okay on regular everyday things, but we couldn't discuss what I really needed to talk about."

Being an only child can be doubly hard in times of

family problems. Brothers and sisters tend to band together to comfort one another (at least temporarily) when a parent dies. But only children are on their own.

When Mary Ann's father died, there were no relatives to be with the family. Mary Ann says, "My mom is not the type to cry in front of anyone. After Dad died, she never broke down once when people were at our house. Oh, I know she cried because I could hear her in her room, but whenever I knocked, she would have stopped crying when she opened the door. That really didn't help me much, but what could I say?"

Mary Ann turned to her best friend, Sandy, and Sandy's mother to get rid of her own grief. "They would talk about Dad and say some of the nice things they remembered about him, and pretty soon I would start crying and maybe they would too. But at least I could get my feelings out in the open with them."

It is important to grieve when someone you love has died, finding the way that suits you best even if it's not the way other members of the family are reacting.

It is all right to cry, get angry, be noisy, or be quiet. Facing your sorrow may mean finding a place to be alone or finding someone to be with. Thinking about your loss, talking about it, writing about it, singing about it, letting it out are the only ways you'll ever be able to get on with life. Without brothers or sisters, there is a possibility that you will have to turn to someone outside your home to help you face your feelings.

If you need a book that talks about death, your library may have *Endings: A Book About Death* by Buff Bradley (Addison-Wesley Publishing Co., 1979).

Grandparents

One big advantage to being an only child is having grandparents all to yourself.

Grandparents' time, energy, and love don't have to be shared, except with cousins, who would be there whether you had a brother or sister or not.

Sometimes your grandparents urge your parents to have more children or scold them because they don't. This is no reflection on the only child. In fact, it might be a compliment.

Grandparents love grandchildren. If you are an extra good or pleasant person, they might feel they would like to have a dozen children just like you around. Sometimes they don't stop to think of the problems or reasons your parents had for limiting the family. Grandparents tend to forget what it means to be a parent of a growing child. If they nag your parents to have more children it is not because they don't approve of you and think your parents could do better. If that were the case, they would be worried about your parents having more children.

Another reason grandparents want many grandchildren is that children tend to keep them young. As long as there are several little ones running around, they don't feel old. But as your parents get older and as *you* get older, this reminds them that they, too, are getting older, and that is difficult for some people to face.

Cousins

If your mother or father or both have a sister or brother, and if that sister or brother has a child, then that child is your cousin.

Having cousins has many advantages. They are family, so they share family joys and family sadnesses. They also have memories and relatives that are the same as yours. Since families try to stay together, you will probably not lose contact with your cousins even if they live a long way from you. Maybe *you* don't write letters to your cousins, but your parents will probably write or phone to learn family news.

But maybe you don't have cousins.

People who study families have made an interesting discovery: An only child often marries another only child. *And* an only child often has only one child. This means that since you are an only child, there is a possibility that your parents were only children. If that is the case, there is no way you can have any aunts, uncles, or cousins.

Perfect Parents

If your parents are perfect—absolutely perfect—you probably already know that they don't use the wrong fork, don't get sick, and don't bleed.

Most parents, however, are human and they are *not* perfect. They have opinions, likes and dislikes, bad days, bad moods, and a temper.

If you live with two parents, you have to cope with two persons' human traits. People with brothers and sisters have to live with even *more* human traits.

Most likely, you, too, are human (isn't everybody?) and have disagreeable traits.

Everyone sometimes has trouble getting along with parents. Only children have more time with their parents, so that they can understand and know one another, but anyone is bound to get ideas parents don't agree with. There will be wants, likes, or dislikes that parents won't go along with.

Sometimes these conflicting ideas are suggested by a friend. Sometimes they come from something you hear on TV or on the radio. Sometimes they are your own thoughts. But if your parents are not in agreement, there is going to be an argument.

Adoptive Parents

At one time people who adopted one child were encouraged to adopt another.

Today, fewer babies are available for adoption, and

many couples cannot adopt a second child.

An adopted only child is no different from a natural only child, but might have a few different problems.

When a couple applies to adopt a baby, they probably have waited a very long time. They plan a very long time. They hope a very long time.

When the child finally joins the family, the parents often try to be perfect. They may think they have to "earn" the child's love. They may be more permissive or discipline less. These actions are only a way of trying to show their love.

Another problem might be curiosity about biological or natural parents. *Some* adoptive parents with only one child fear losing that one child's love to the natural parents if they are ever united. Communication—talking—is the best solution to this problem, but this may take the help of someone outside the family.

Family Relationships

There are six relationships in a family with one child:

1. Mother with father
2. Father with mother
3. Mother with child
4. Child with mother
5. Father with child
6. Child with father

There are twelve relationships in a family with two children! Twice as many personality combinations:

1. Mother with father
2. Father with mother
3. Mother with Child A
4. Mother with Child B
5. Father with Child A
6. Father with Child B
7. Child A with mother
8. Child B with mother
9. Child A with father
10. Child B with father
11. Child A with Child B
12. Child B with Child A

No Family Is Perfect

Whatever the makeup of the one-child family, the parents have probably been asked at least one of these dumb questions:

- Do you really think you're being fair to the child to raise him (or her) without brothers and sisters?
- Why did you stop at one child?
- When are you going to have another one?
- Won't he (or she) be terribly spoiled?
- Aren't you being awfully selfish?

This is the kind of flack the parents of an only child must face.

One thing parents have to give up when they have only one child is a companion for their child.

One mother of four children says, "Our kids have never had a boring moment. One of them always has an idea for a new game or activity."

Only children, however, look to their parents to play games with them, to entertain them, to go places with them, to talk to them. In other words, parents of only children have to act as siblings (brothers and sisters) as well as mother and father.

While anyone knows that sisters and brothers seldom get along, they at least put up with one another.

On a camping trip, they can explore the woods together—not always in peace and harmony, but at least together.

At a movie, they go and return together. But an only child has no companion other than parents or people outside the family. So parents have to fill the role of both parent *and* sister or brother.

But there are advantages to being an only child. Tracy says, "My folks and I are a lot closer than my friends are to their parents. Whenever my friend Tasha wants to talk to her mom, there is almost always a sister hanging around listening. But I can talk to my mother anytime. And she always has time to listen to me. She's not off changing a diaper or putting a bandage on someone's knee or settling an argument between brothers."

Is there a perfect way to grow up? Is having an older brother or a younger brother (or both) a perfect

Parents and Other Kinds of Family 41

situation? Is having a younger sister perfect? Is having an older sister perfect? Is having . . . ?

The list is endless, and no situation is perfect because life is not perfect.

5
A Friend Is Someone Who . . .

A friend is someone who can do some things better than you, some things the same as you, and at least one thing not as well as you. In other words, a friend is someone who doesn't want a friend (you) who is perfect!

Only children learn early that friends are important, and they will treat each friend as a very important person.

Sharing or Selfish

Little children are naturally selfish. They won't share toys. They won't share treats. They won't even share their brussels sprouts.

"You should have more than one child so they will learn to share," someone is always saying to parents of only children.

With that thinking, it must be true that all children who have brothers or sisters automatically share. And if they don't automatically share when they are small, by the time they are eleven years old, they have certainly learned to share everything.

Is that what you have noticed? Probably not. Hav-

A Friend Is Someone Who ...

ing a brother or sister usually makes a child *not* want to share. A brother or sister can drive a child to hoarding toys, hiding treasures, and never sharing!

A mother might say, "Share your toy with your little brother." If the little brother gets a chance at the toy, it's because the older child obeyed, not shared.

Sharing usually comes from a feeling of trust. Often only children have found the world trustworthy. Their parents have been fair with them. Their early experiences with other children were fair. And as they get older, they learn that to be treated fairly you have to be fair. So the only child often bypasses the "selfish" phase.

Of course there are selfish only children, just as there are children with brothers and sisters who are generous, but the only child usually has not learned to be grabby.

Bossy

A boss is the person your father or mother works for who can make your parent crabby, grouchy, and mean after work. Why? Because that person may make difficult demands on your parent. That person may pile work on your parent. That person may be hard to work for.

When children play together, they figure out different things to do. Sometimes they do what one person wants. Sometimes they do what another person wants. As Big Bird used to tell us when we watched *Sesame Street*, this is called cooperation.

At other times, when children play together, they figure out different things to do, but they always end up doing what the bossy one wants to do. This is not called fair, not called cooperation, and definitely not the way to keep a friend!

Your parent probably has to put up with the boss because of the need for a job and money.

But when children play together, it is because they like what they are doing and have fun. When it stops being fun, they find someone else to play with. There is no reason to play with someone when it's not fun.

Some only children learn this too late. Some only children are allowed to help make decisions with their parents. Because they are onlies, their opinions are valued by their parents. They are allowed to "boss" once in a while. But they have trouble seeing that friendships are different. Others may not give a hoot about an only child's opinions or wishes.

When only children get used to having things their way at home, they might try to force friends to do things their way. Soon they have ex-friends, former friends, and finally no friends.

Friendship has to be equal give-and-take. One time one friend makes a decision, the next time the other gets a chance to make a choice.

Substitute Brother or Sister

There are substitutions by the jillion in the world today: substitute sweeteners, substitute teachers, substitute sale items at the discount store, substitute players in a football game.

For years, only children have adopted substitute brothers or sisters.

Many only children feel they are missing something by not having brothers or sisters. They feel as if there is an empty spot that needs to be filled. So, they pick someone to be a substitute brother or sister.

There is an advantage to this procedure of filling up the family. The only child can pick a friend with whom he or she gets along—few fights, few smashed belongings, few major problems. If the substitute turns out to be less than desirable, a replacement can be found. (Try doing that with a *real* brother or sister!)

The substitute can fill the role of brother or sister, go on family outings, spend time at home, attend family birthday parties, and almost be a member of the family. At the same time, the substitute brother or sister doesn't cost the only child's parents much. Of course, the substitute's *real* parents provide basic needs like food, clothing, medical and dental needs, school fees, and pet food.

How Friendships Grow

We plant a seed to grow a tree. Friendship is just like a tree. If it is planted in a good base (like a seed in good soil), it will grow strong.

At first you are careful not to offend your friend, just as you are careful to protect the fragile sprout of the tree.

With time, however, your friendship grows strong. Just as the tree will weather rain, hail, and snowstorms, your friendship will weather arguments, fights, changing interests, and new friends.

Trees can last many years. Friendship, too, can last many years. Right now it is probably hard to think of yourself as an adult, and it is hard to think of your friend as a grown-up. But you will both grow up, and your friendship might last through the years.

Lots of people as old as your parents or grandparents still have a friend they met in elementary school. Friends are a very important part of the only child's life.

How to Treat Friends

Rules are strange. Few people enjoy sitting around reading the rules to a game. But without rules, no one would win. In fact, there wouldn't even be a game without rules. There are rules for getting along with friends. Without the rules, there won't be any friends.

A Friend Is Someone Who . . .

- Imagination is fun, but lies are not funny. Honesty is basic to friendship—no making up stories, no making events sound better than they really are.
- Thoughtfulness about money helps. Your friend's family may not have as much money to spend as yours might have. Keep this in mind.
- Friendship cannot be bought. The difference between sharing and buying is complicated. Buying a friendship is using money or things to get someone to be your friend.

Here are two examples:

Story 1: Two boys are walking down the street.
CHRIS: I'd like to go to a movie.
SHAWN: Me too.
CHRIS: But I don't have any money.
SHAWN: I do! I'll treat us to a show if you'll help me wash my dad's car.

This is a story of sharing. If Chris will share the work, Shawn will share his money.

Story 2: Two boys are walking down the street.
MARTY: I think I'll go play soccer.
TONY: I don't want to.
MARTY: Well, I do. I'll see you later.
TONY: I've got some money. I'll treat you to a movie if you don't go play soccer.

This is a story of buying friendship. In story 1, Shawn was sharing, even sort of letting Chris earn the money. In story 2, Tony was buying friendship, bribing Marty to go with him instead of playing soccer.

- No one is perfect—no mistakes, no spilled juice, no bad habits, no forgotten chores, no cavities and no warts, no poor grades. Friends aren't perfect either.
- Admitting you are wrong and laughing at your mistakes helps.
- A friend may prefer the peace and quiet of your home to the zoo at his or her own house. Tranquillity should be shared.

Some more suggestions:

- Trust your friend and be trustworthy.
- Take baths at least once every two years.
- Say what's on your mind, but say it nicely.
- Walk a mile in your friend's shoes. (Look at things from his or her point of view.)
- Don't give live snakes or dead chickens as birthday gifts.
- Think before you say or do something. Don't be a klutz. Could your friend's feelings be hurt? Don't take a chance.
- Say you are sorry when you make a mistake.
- When the biggest secret of the century (or any other secret) has been confided to you, *don't tell*.

A Friend Is Someone Who . . .

- Keep your cat's litterbox tidy.
- Don't talk about your friends behind their backs, unless you can say something good.
- Don't be demanding.
- Return ski poles, sweaters, comic books promptly or don't borrow in the first place. (Except bubble gum. You probably shouldn't return that at all.)
- Try to be easy for your friend to be around. Moodiness seems to be some people's trademark. If it's yours, think about your moods.
- Don't take advantage of your friend.
- Respect your friend's need to be alone sometimes.
- *Never* say anything bad about your friend's brothers or sisters. Even if your friend says some terrible things, just listen. Brothers and sisters get angry with one another, but they really do love one another.
- Don't brag. Bragging is boring:
  "I have three ski jackets."
  "I have four bikes."
  "I have five dogs."
  "I have thirty-seven hamsters."
  "I have all the money in the world."
- One brag usually encourages someone else's brag. Don't start it:
  "I can jog a mile without resting."
  "I can swim thirty laps at once."

"I can beat anyone at tennis."

"I can get kicked out of the library without even trying."

- Don't show off. Showing off is almost as bad as bragging.
- Don't pass judgment. Friends are fair with each other. Hear the whole story before you believe gossip. Sometimes people have reasons for doing things that cannot be expressed openly or at a certain time.
- Have the courage to do what is right. An only child probably has more chances to talk with parents and learn about life and its dangers than children who come from families where every minute is taken up with diapers, laundry, and crying babies. Only children are usually respected by their friends. It's a responsibility.
- Listen. Friends are for understanding. The best friends have time or take time to listen and to talk.

Most only children value the time they get to spend with another child. Since there are no other children living in their house, they are glad to share their possessions, cooperate, and be a friend.

Parents as Friends

The friendship of parents is an advantage of being an only child. There is more time for being together and more opportunities for parents to know and understand a lone offspring.

In a family where there is only one parent, that parent might want to be the child's best friend. While there is nothing wrong with being friends with parents, it is important to have friends your own age.

Onlies can build friendship by inviting classmates home to play, to eat dinner, to stay overnight.

Moms and dads can't really share worries about a test coming up at school. *They* don't have to take the test. They can't share feelings about teachers or problems with other students. *They* don't have to be there taking the teacher's rough assignments or listening to classmates. It is right to tell parents about feelings and problems, but it is also important to have friends your own age who are going through the same things.

There should be time for both—friendship with parents and friends your own age.

Older Friends

Many only children live around more adults than children. Perhaps their neighborhood is all older people. Friends of the family might be adults who don't have children living at home.

From a very young age, some only children can talk to older people (even very old people) and are interested in the same things as older people. When young people are around older people, they learn that wrinkles mean something. Older people, because they are older, can share a lot of information, stories, and excitement from their long lives.

Loss of a Friend

Things happen.

Parents move and take you along.

Or the other child's parents move and take the friend along.

This doesn't have to mean THE END to that friendship. Friends can write letters or exchange cassette tapes. They can share newspaper clippings or souvenirs. Although TV commercials say long-distance telephoning is cheap, that's not always true. Long-distance phone calls can be expensive, so parents' permission should be asked before calling.

Sometimes other things happen:

- Friends change and lose interest in activities or subjects they have always enjoyed together.
- A big fight ends the friendship.
- One friend has grown up faster than the other one.
- One friend finds a new best friend.
- Your interests change in opposite directions.
- One friend does or says things the other doesn't like.

To lose a friend is probably harder on an only child, since a friend has been a very important part of everyday life.

What to do?

Parents really are best friends, so an only can turn to them—but not forever!

It's worth the effort to get into situations where new friends may be: groups, sports, clubs, musical activities, church organizations, Scouts, space cadets.

New Friends

For the new kid on the block or the new kid in school, making friends is probably not the easiest thing in the world. But it's hard for anyone to go into something unfamiliar. With zero brothers and sisters or with twenty, it's always hard to be "new."

It's hard for Dad to start a new job or for Mom to join a new group. It's hard for grandparents to pull up their roots and move to a new part of the country or to a retirement home.

But on the whole, change is good. It gives people a new view of life. So any young person moving or changing schools might as well face facts. There are going to be some hard times, but meeting them head-on is better than hiding under the bed and hoping they'll go away. (They won't.) Here are some ways of meeting people in the new school or the new neighborhood:

- Be available. Don't always be in such a hurry at school that no one can say anything to you.
- Be visible. At home, find something to do outside where people can see you and invite you to join in their activities. Even sitting on the porch reading a book is better than hiding behind the window curtains peeking out!
- Find something interesting to do and invite a neighbor to join in.
- Get involved. See pages 67–70 for more ideas.

No one can be good at everything, so it's no disgrace to try something and fail. Besides, this provides a chance for a friend to be better at something. One can win a friend by being the first to admire what someone has accomplished.

6
Feelings–How to Tame Them

How do you feel about being an only child?

There are all sorts of feelings people have about being only children. How you feel is not so important as knowing yourself.

Try talking to yourself—preferably in your room or someplace where you will have privacy. Self-conversations in public places make people stare!

How Do You Feel Today?

No one feels the same every day. Some days you may feel very angry. Some days you may feel ashamed. Other days you may be very glad to be an only child. It's almost like being two people, one person bored and tired of being an only, the other actually enjoying it.

Angry

Lisa, at fourteen, expressed a feeling of anger at being an only child. "I go over to Peggy's house and see all the kids. Most of them are adopted. Some are racially mixed and two are handicapped. It just makes me mad that my folks are so selfish that they won't adopt another kid."

Deirdre, too, feels angry. "I get kind of mad," she says. "The only reason I don't have brothers or sisters is because of my mother's job. That job is more important to her than anything. I really wish I had a brother or sister. I wouldn't care how terrible he or she was. I just wish I wasn't an only child."

Jealous

Kevin, age eleven, is often jealous of his friends with brothers and sisters. "Oh, sure," Kevin says, "they fight and everything like that. But when one kid gets yelled at and maybe sent to his room, the other kids are there sympathizing and being on his side. Not so at my house. If I get sent to my room, I'm there by myself."

Some days it seems as if everyone else in the world has a brother or a sister or both. Frank is going to a ball game with his big brother. Eric and his little sister are going to their grandmother's house. Everyone else has a companion.

When you get to feeling this way, it's time to turn to Chapter 12 and remind yourself of the advantages of being an only child. Then turn to pages 67–70 and think about some things to get involved in.

Of course, it's not always easy to be an only child. But then, someone with a sister or a brother will tell you it's not easy to have another child in the family either!

Ashamed

Some people feel ashamed of being an only child. Sheila feels this way. "I'm ashamed of it sometimes," Sheila says. "We go to a church where just about everyone has lots of kids. All my friends are from big families. Whenever I tell someone I am an only child, they kind of look at me like I'm strange or something."

Lonely

When Jason is sitting alone in his room thinking about his father who died, he hates being an only child. "There's no one to talk to," he says. "I feel so all alone. Even to have someone to fight with would be a relief."

Everyone is lonely sometimes. Old people are lonely. Neighbors are lonely.

The best cure for loneliness is to get involved in something or to invite someone to visit. Curing your loneliness may also cure someone else's loneliness. Try it!

Glad

Not everyone dislikes being an only. Thirteen-year-old Jay says, "I'm glad I'm an only child. I think what I like best is all the things I can do with my folks that we couldn't do if I had a brother or sister—both because we couldn't afford it and also because a littler kid couldn't do the mountain climbing we do."

Sarah agrees with Jay. "I'm glad to be an only

child," Sarah says, "especially when I come home from Debbie's house. It's a relief to get into the peace and quiet of my own room. Debbie has two little brothers, and those kids are always either fighting or snooping into Debbie's things or making more noise than six kids."

Come to Terms with Your Feelings

Right or wrong, legitimate or not, it is important for all children to have feelings about their life and to think about these feelings. Once you have faced the way you feel about the situation, you can understand how someone else might feel.

Some people dislike being an only child so much and feel so tortured that they vow never to do the same thing to their own child.

Others simply accept their life. They realize there is nothing they can do to alter the situation, so they just make the best of it.

Still others really like being an only child. While they sometimes complain, they really enjoy the advantages they have.

But no matter how one feels, it is important not to hide the feelings—to control them, yes, but not to conceal them.

More disadvantages and advantages are listed in Chapters 11 and 12, but you may have particular disadvantages or special advantages. It's helpful to make a list of each, writing them out on paper. Give them a number value, if you wish, and add up the points for the disadvantages and the advantages.

Once you have examined your own feelings and have gotten to know yourself, there is one more important step—coming to terms with your feelings and learning to cope with your emotions.

Surprisingly, feelings change. The way you feel today may be very different from the way you will feel next week or next month.

You cannot change things. If you are an only child, you will probably be one the rest of your life, so it's a good idea to accept your life as it stands.

Do Something

With strong negative feelings like anger or loneliness or shame or jealousy, it helps to talk to someone. If parents don't seem to be appropriate, perhaps another relative or a friend of the family or a teacher or a counselor or a religious leader will listen. Talking out problems will not only make them easier to live with, it might make them go away!

7
Alone Is Not Lonely

Damion just about drove his mother nuts last summer.

"I'm bored."

"There's no one to hang around with."

"Want to play ball, Mom?"

"There's no one to pick on."

Damion is not an only chld, and that is why he was such a pest. His younger brother was having a turn spending two weeks with their grandparents.

Even though they don't realize it or appreciate it, children with brothers or sisters come to depend on each other for entertainment of some kind, even if it is irritating.

Only children learn to cope from the beginning. They have never had another youngster around all the time, so they don't expect to have someone else to imagine, to create, to plan, to play, or to work with.

Alone or Lonely?

"Lonely" is a common description of only children. Most people who are *not* only children think of only children as lonely. But there is a big difference

Alone Is Not Lonely

between being alone and being lonely.

"Lonely" is supposed to mean "sad for the lack of companionship."

All people are lonely at one time or another, whether they are only children or have brothers and sisters. There is something crazy about loneliness. Of course you may feel lonely when you're all by yourself in your bedroom, but you can also feel lonely when you're at a party or when you're in a crowd at a shopping center or when you're in school.

Being alone does not necessarily mean being sad. Being alone is simply not having anyone around, and it can be great. Alone times are times to grow, to dream, and to get to know yourself.

Read. Write. Watch a spider.

Do art work. Take a walk. Study a word atlas.

Cut your fingernails.

Everyone should learn to love quiet and make an effort to be alone sometimes.

Privacy

Everybody needs privacy.

Most people need privacy when they are taking a bath. Some need it when they have something to think about or a decision to make.

Only children usually have all the privacy they need, since there are no brothers or sisters to be pests.

Only children can keep a diary, but many children

with brothers or sisters need to use a secret code to keep their diary private.

Only children can make a special gift for a parent and keep it a secret. It's not so easy for a child with brothers and sisters.

Creativity

Studies show that many only children grow up to use their creativity: perhaps by becoming writers, artists, sculptors, musicians, inventors.

Because of the alone time as a child, these children have been able to stimulate their creativity. It is never too late to begin.

Chapter 13 mentions some famous only children. Many became known for their creativity.

Fantasy World

Dolls, stuffed animals, or other tools of imagination may play an important part in the world of the only child longer than they do in larger families. These toys are friends. They will listen to troubles. They are always there. This is probably why A. A. Milne's books about Winnie the Pooh are so popular—even with adults. Christopher Robin, who was an only child, certainly enjoyed and related to the stuffed animals in his life.

A fantasy world can be a lot of fun. When you were small, it was called make-believe or pretend.

There is no harm in imagination or fantasy, as long as you know you are dreaming. Using a fantasy world as an escape is not harmful *unless* you have trouble

Alone Is Not Lonely

telling the difference between the real world and your fantasies *or* if you prefer your fantasy world to the real world and begin to keep yourself away from your friends or family just so you can live in the world of your imagination.

Then you need to ask for help from one of your parents or a teacher or counselor.

As long as you can limit your fantasy-world dreaming to appropriate times, enjoy it. Few children with brothers or sisters are afforded the luxury of such fun!

Many only children fantasize about having a brother or a sister. Paula, age twelve, dreamed about her imaginary big brother. "He would take me to the basketball games with him," she said, "and all his friends would want to talk to me. But he would be very protective and only let me talk with the best one."

Twelve-year-old Larry always wanted a little brother. "We would play ball together," Larry says, "and go fishing together, and he would look up to me and ask me questions. It would be great. I guess it would make me feel important."

Almost every only child who wishes for a brother or sister fantasizes that they would genuinely like each other, defend each other, and have a close friendship.

Life is not like that very often. Kids are kids. Even if *you* cared about your brother or sister, there is no guarantee that person would care about you. He or she might be jealous or destructive, tell lies or blame you when something is not your fault, or a million other things.

Fantasies are fun, but real life is seldom as nice and comfortable as a dream world.

Adoption is another thing only children often fantasize about. Since there are no brothers or sisters for them to look like, they may convince themselves that they are adopted. On bad days, they may fantasize that there is a "real" parent somewhere who is going to return and rescue them.

Pets

A dog, a cat, a rabbit, a hamster, a horse, a koala bear, an elephant—these are terrific companions.

Unfortunately not all life-styles and not all parents permit an animal. But if yours do, enjoy it.

An only child will usually take better responsibility for an animal than will a child from a home where there are other children. There are several reasons:

- There is no brother or sister to take care of the animal, no one to dump the responsibility on.
- Only children are generally more responsible.
- There are no distractions—no brothers or sisters to make the responsible owner forget to take care of the animal.
- Only children are generally more concerned about a pet, since it is their *only* companion and it is theirs alone.

Alone Is Not Lonely

Television

If you have ever been to a live golf tournament, or watched a golf tournament on TV, you know that golf pros get exercise, fame, and money.

Meanwhile, TV viewers get blurred vision, little or no exercise, and the desire to spend their own money on whatever is advertised during the commercial breaks.

When a golf tournament is over, the audience finds something else to do. But when a TV show is over, the television moneymongers quickly provide another intriguing title to lure viewers through yet another hour of the TV stare syndrome.

In a house with lots of children, the TV set might go off sooner for a multitude of reasons:

- One child finds something else interesting to do and the others join in.
- One child wants Channel 4 and the other wants Channel 7. The ensuing argument leads a parent to turn the TV set off.
- Two (or more) children make enough racket to drive a parent bananas. The additional noise of a TV set is often too much.
- The TV set is allowed on only during certain hours to ensure that all family members will get their chores and homework finished.

In an only child's home, television might be noise, artificial imagination, and fights: in other words, a substitute sibling (brother or sister). Television has been called an always available baby-sitter.

Sometimes young people without brothers or sisters depend on the TV set to be their companion. That can be good or bad. Television can be a great part of life—depending on how you use it.

While you are watching the tube, it's fun to do something else as well (not homework!). You can exercise, work a crossword puzzle or a jigsaw puzzle, write a letter to a friend or a relative. To make commercials more interesting, turn off the sound and think up new dialogue to fit the action. Or figure out your own endings for the story or the commercials.

How much television do you watch?

Is your one claim to fame the fact that you have seen every rerun of *The Brady Bunch* twice?

Most areas of the country now have great programs available—educational specials, musical presentations, instructional or accredited programs.

The viewer should ask: Am I learning something useful from this electronic box? How often am I depending on it for relaxation? Is the TV set my live-in baby-sitter?

Bored?

Are you bored? Is there nothing to do?

This is the way the world works.

Bored people are always bored because they never make anything interesting happen. Some people go through their entire lives being bored, and they are usually boring to be around.

But once bored people make something interesting happen, they aren't bored, or boring, anymore.

There are lots of ways to make something interesting happen.

Challenging Time-Takers

You could watch your toenails grow, but there are better things to do.

You can become an expert on:

- Bubble gum (how many companies make bubble gum?)
- Fireworks (who invented fireworks?)
- Golf balls (what's inside a golf ball?)
- Your favorite animal (the octopus has three hearts; the shrew must eat every hour or two, or it will starve to death)
- New words (start with obscurantism, funicular, and zoophyte)
- A famous person—dead or alive
- An industry (how many shoe stores are there in the United States? how many companies manufacture magnets?)

Do you like to work with your hands? Crafts are fun to do, and the end product can make a nice gift. Try needlework (knitting, crocheting, needlepoint, macramé, embroidery, batik, weaving, quilting). Kits are available to help you get started in leatherwork, wood engraving, assembling models, or stained glass. Other crafts include pottery, woodworking, and whittling.

Collections are interesting to make grow. Some are a real challenge to find, such as unusual names of people, newspaper typographical mistakes, or pictures of unusual animals. Stamps, rocks, butterflies, bottle caps, buttons, or banks might be easier to collect. Or see how many inflated (blown-up) balloons it takes to fill your bedroom.

Hobbies can be interesting for an entire lifetime. You may enjoy taking photographs, entering contests, launching model rockets, flying model planes, or setting up a model railroad.

There are clubs for all kinds of interests. If you enjoy a hobby, there is probably an organization of other people who are also interested in that hobby. Or you could join a Scout troop, the Y, a community theater, a computer club, 4-H, the Civil Air Patrol Cadet Program, or a church group.

Lessons are offered in many fascinating things, such as sign language, chess, music (vocal or instrumental), art (drawing, watercolors, oil painting, charcoal, sculpture), crafts, cooking, or yoga.

Sports are not only fun, they are good for physical fitness. You might have fun swimming, bowling, roller-skating, ice-skating, bicycle racing, or dancing (ballet, tap dance, square dance, or aerobic dance). Or try tennis, golf, judo, karate, gymnastics, trampolining, or soccer.

If just going somewhere sounds like fun, go by bicycle, hike, take a bus tour, or go on horseback. Go to the library, an art gallery, a museum, or tour a business or an industry.

To get a really nice feeling inside, help someone. Volunteer at a nursing home, a child-care center, a hospital, through a church, as a junior fire fighter, through the Red Cross or Salvation Army, at a political organization, or for an ecological or a conservation group.

You might offer to read or write letters for blind people, help provide physical therapy for disabled people in their home, or raise puppies to be trained to lead the blind.

You can go visit someone who you know is lonely —maybe an elderly neighbor or a physically disabled person who cannot leave home.

Do you like to get mail? You can send for free things. There are books available listing free or low-cost items to send for. Ask at the library for the current edition of *Free Stuff for Kids* by Bruce Lansky (Meadowbrook Press).

Other people like to get mail too (and besides, they might write back). Send a letter to a pen pal, grandparent, favorite author, or favorite singer, TV personality, or movie star. Tell a magazine editor what you think of an article or a story, or let a government official know your opinion on a political issue.

And before putting pen and paper away, try some fun writing. Write a story, a poem, a book, or start a diary. Compose the music or write the words for a song.

The best way to relax or to learn something new is to read! Try a fantasy book, a science-fiction book, a mystery, a Western, or a romance. Discover something new in an interesting facts book or a how-to book.

You don't have to be bored or be boring!

Useful Money-makers

Most people need money, including children. An allowance helps, but there are other ways to collect money.

You can get jobs in your neighborhood. Paint fences, mailboxes, or outdoor furniture. Do yard work—rake leaves, weed gardens, mow, trim, and water lawns. Shovel snow, wash cars, or wash windows.

You can help people having garage sales: offer to answer their phone and take messages, hang and un-hang signs, help set up tables, help price items before the sale, entertain their small children during the sale, fix their lunch during the sale, wrap and box unsold items after the sale.

Or you can have your own yard sale and sell old toys and outgrown clothing.

When neighbors go on vacation, someone has to care for their houseplants. You can offer to go to the neighbors' homes or bring their plants to your home to care for them.

Pets, too, need attention. Dogs need to be walked, bathed, and fed, especially while the owners are on trips. And many pet owners are anxious to find someone to use the pooper-scooper on a weekly basis.

If your neighbors have small children, you might tutor them or walk them to and from day camp. Try putting on magic shows, clown acts, or puppet shows for the children's birthday parties or being available to take pictures at the party, serve refreshments, and clean up spills. Mothers are often happy to have an extra helper.

If you have a large bedroom, parents of young children might "rent" a shelf or the corner of your room to hide their children's gifts just before Christmas or birthdays.

While it's nice to do things for handicapped people just to be helpful, many people who are confined to their homes are able to pay to have someone run errands or do chores around the house.

If you live near a business area, many businesses might use your services. Very small offices often need someone to run errands, such as buying supplies, taking papers to a copy service, or delivering mail or packages to the post office.

Furniture stores hire young people to dust furniture and vacuum carpeting. Clothing or department stores occasionally need young fashion models. Car agencies need someone to clean the cars on the lot. And grocery stores hire sackers and shelf stockers.

Of course, there are always handbills, circulars,

and newspapers to deliver.

If you live near a fishing area, dig and sell worms to fishermen. Or if you live in a rural area, clean stables and (with the owner's permission, of course) sell the manure to home gardeners. Farmers and ranchers usually have chores for young people to do.

Most areas of the country now have redemption centers for recycling. If there is a collection point nearby, gather aluminum, glass, cans, and newspapers and sell them for recycling.

Check with your parents before you begin any money-making projects, but with a little imagination you will find ways to earn money!

8
It's Not Always Easy

Chores

Mrs. Jensen, the mother of two, has a chart on the refrigerator door. The chart shows whose turn it is to vacuum, whose turn it is to wash dishes, get the trash bagged and on the curb, fix the salad, clean the bathroom, and so on.

Many only children complain that they have to do *all* the chores. They feel sorry for themselves because there is no sister or brother to take a turn. Usually, however, the only child's parents are doing the sister's or brother's chores and sharing the burden.

Few parents actually ask their children to do too much, but if you really and truly feel you are being overworked, you might ask yourself these questions:

1. Is either of my parents seriously ill or absent from our home?
2. Do both my parents work outside the home? (Or, in a one-parent home, Does my parent work outside the home?) Do they have time to do the chores I feel I shouldn't have to do?
3. Do my chores interfere with doing my home-

work? (Of course, this would mean no time for TV, no phone calls, no time with friends, no sports—just work, work, work from the minute you get home from school till you go to bed.)

If you still feel you have too many chores, try making a written list of everything you are expected to do. Then sit down with your parents and discuss (don't argue!) what you think you should have to do, asking them why they feel it is necessary for you to do more.

Sometimes chores *seem* awful and people spend more time worrying and talking about them than actually doing them. There are ways to make your own chores more interesting and fun. Try these suggestions and then discover your own tricks:

- Listen to music or a cassette while you wash dishes.
- Tape a string to the trash bag and get your cat to chase the string while you collect the trash from around the house.
- Sing while you vacuum.
- Make up silly rhymes or silly songs about the chore you are doing.
- Time yourself and try to set a speed record. Each time you do the chore, try to do it faster, but don't skimp on doing a good job!

It's Not Always Easy 75

Difficult Times

Some times are more difficult than others to be an only child.

After school you may have someone over to your house or you may have activities, but evenings can be harder.

In some quiet neighborhoods, summers seem very long and boring to an only child.

Again, get busy and you'll probably never have time to be lonely.

Joining In

Many only children find it harder to join organizations or clubs than do young people with brothers or sisters. Some onlies hesitate to get involved in parties, games, school outings, or team sports.

Instead, they prefer one friend for an overnight stay or one-person competition such as tennis.

It may be easy for someone to scold and say, "You should . . . you should . . . you should . . ." And it may be easy to agree, saying, "Yes, I really should. . . ."

But taking the plunge is harder. Actually doing something new is difficult, and avoiding it doesn't make it easier.

Try starting in slowly.

If you were going swimming in a cold lake, you probably wouldn't jump off the dock into freezing water. You would start by putting a toe in the water and then wading in up to your waist.

You can do the same thing with friendships or activities.

Get to know one person at a time. Meet one, invite him or her to your house, exchange visits. Then meet another person and become friends.

Waiting for a perfect time doesn't work. There is never a perfect time. As soon as you decide to do something, don't put it off. Do it right away. Meet someone. Join a group. The longer you wait, the more you will worry, and the less likely you are ever to get involved.

Some people without brothers or sisters grow up feeling very important because that is the way their parents have treated them. The only child is naturally the most important child in a family. Then when that person gets in a group with others, he or she is suddenly just another child—not president, not captain, not the leader. It is hard for many only children to adjust to not being the most important.

Separation

Very often, only children find it hard to do anything without their parents. All their lives, they have been included in most of their parents' activities. Breaking away may be more difficult than for a child from a large family.

Of course, no one is suggesting that you join the Army when you are eight years old, but eight (or earlier) is a good time to be a little independent. You might spend a night at a school friend's house or at the home of some of your parents' adult friends, or stay overnight with aunts, uncles, cousins, or grandparents.

When Miranda spent her first night away from home, she admits, "Betty's mom let us stay up really late, *and* we got to watch a TV show my folks won't let me watch. It was sure a surprise to see that other kids don't live the same way I do."

Some things require more adjustment than others. A long stay away from home might be a little more difficult than a one-night stay. Educational tours, trips with friends, or summer camp might entail being away for a week or longer. When you're away from the familiar place, the food is different, the routine is different, and the noises in the night are different. But they are not forever. The education you can get from such a trip is worth a little homesickness.

The experience will be a challenge and fun. You will have a chance to show your parents and yourself that you can take care of yourself. You *can!*

All Alone in the World?

Some people rely on their brothers or sisters for support. Sometimes they depend on each other for money; sometimes, for reassurance that they are doing the right thing or are doing a good job; sometimes, for company.

These people will often say it is too bad that an only child has no brothers or sisters. But you may notice that they don't start to brag about something their own brother or sister has done.

Sure, there are disadvantages of being an only child. Chapter 11 lists some of them.

But only children are not necessarily all alone in the world. Because they need others' friendship and put a high value on it, they often make better friends. Onlies learn to look at their work or their actions and *know* for themselves whether they are doing a good job. Onlies have the whole world and all its people at their feet.

Independence

Sometimes parents of only children can't let go of their children as easily as parents who have more than one. They don't let their only child do things independently as young as children with brothers or sisters are allowed to do things. Since the parents have no other children to compare with, they might not be aware that the only is ready for a little independence.

Since the parents have no younger children, they have no one else to worry about, so they sometimes end up concentrating all their worries and attachments on the one child.

If your parents are this way, treat them kindly. But explain that you feel you can handle a certain responsibility—*not* just because someone else is doing it, but because you are aware of the circumstances involved.

If they refuse, try to find something halfway you can all agree you are ready to do.

9
Who's Spoiled?

Through the years, only children have been labeled by one term that is supposed to apply to all of them: SPOILED.

Are you spoiled?

If you have ever smelled a rotten egg, you know the meaning of spoiled. If you smell like a rotten egg, you are undoubtedly spoiled.

If you have ever tasted sour milk, you know the meaning of spoiled. If you taste like soured milk, you are absolutely spoiled.

But "to spoil" is also supposed to mean to damage the disposition by pampering; to indulge or coddle; to cause to expect too much by overindulgence. Does this apply to you?

> Do you whine?
> Do you usually get to have things your own way?
> Do you get privileges you have not earned?
> Do you get privileges you don't deserve?
> Do you demand special privileges?
> Are you self-centered, caring only about yourself?

Are you conceited? Do you think you are fantastically terrific?
Are you selfish?

If your answers are yes, then you are definitely spoiled.

Expectations and Demands

What are your parents' obligations to provide for you? What do you have a right to expect?

As a human being, and too young to earn your own living, you can *expect* these things from your parents:

- Food: A balanced diet. *Chocolate cream pie is a luxury!*
- Shelter: A roof over your head. *It need not be the most beautiful home in town.*
- Medical attention: A doctor's care when you are ill or injured. *Plastic surgery to make you simply gorgeous is not an essential.*
- Dental attention: Adequate dental care. *Cosmetic oral surgery is not an obligation.*
- Clothing: Adequate clothing to keep you warm in winter and relatively comfortable in summer. *A cheerleading uniform or the latest name brand in shoes is not a necessity.*
- Education: Schooling provided by the taxpayers. *A private school is not something you can expect.*

So what else must parents supply?

- An allowance? *This is not an obligation.*
- A telephone? *Even a family telephone is not required.*
- The latest record album or movie? *Neither is essential to sustaining life.*
- The in brand of shoes or designer jeans? *These would be 100 percent luxury.*

Appreciation

You say "thank you" when your parents pass the butter, but how about other times?

Appreciation is not only saying "thanks" out loud, it is also the way you show your thanks. If you get a new sweater, how do you take care of it? Do you keep it clean and neatly folded, or is it stuffed in a bag with a sweaty gym suit for three days? Or is it already lost?

If you get a special dessert, do you wash the dishes without being asked or do you mutter "thanks" and then run back to the TV set?

Material Possessions

When an only child has nice things, it is assumed they demand nice things. And some people think these nice things mean the child is spoiled.

"Things" do not necessarily make a child spoiled. The attitude toward things is what makes the difference.

Most only children have more stuff than their friends who have brothers and sisters. Parents can buy more items for only one child than they could if they had two, three, four, or eleven children.

Clothing of an only child also might be nicer than friends' clothes. Money is part of the reason. Also, younger brothers and sisters wear outgrown clothing from the older children.

But money is not the only reason only children have more things. An only child will probably need more. While a brother and sister will have each other and each other's belongings, an only child will probably need more things to be entertained. If two brothers each have a toy car, they can race those cars. But if an only child has a car, what can it race? The only child needs *two* cars.

The only child will look at these cars as his or her race cars, not *two* race cars. But children from larger families *count.* "I have one race car," they say, "but you have *two* race cars." (They probably learned this by counting chocolate chips in cookies and yelling "Not fair" when a sister gets more chocolate chips.)

There is another reason the only child might have more things.

Only children often are more careful with their possessions. Besides, there are no little sisters to step on things, no little brothers to sit on things, no other children in the family to smash something in anger. Things are generally better cared for and last longer.

Attitude

Being spoiled is an attitude—the way someone looks at life. It doesn't have to be an only child who is spoiled. Many children with brothers and sisters are spoiled—they want, they demand, they feel they are owed something.

Ask yourself some questions:

1. How do you act?
2. How do you express your appreciation?
3. What are you appreciative of?
4. What do you say?
5. What do you do?
6. Do you expect?
7. Do you demand?

Only you can answer these questions. Your answers can tell you whether you're spoiled or not. The rest of the world already knows.

Unspoiling

If a pound of raw hamburger is left on the kitchen counter for two days, it spoils. It smells. It isn't even fit for the dog. And there is no turning it around. There is no way to make it good again.

Luckily, a child is not hamburger. If you have answered the questions above and must admit that you are spoiled, *you* can change.

Here are some ways to start:

- Share. (You decide how.)
- Do something nice for an old person. (You decide what.)
- Do something nice for your parents. (You decide what.)
- Put a black mark on your calendar every time you hear yourself say:

  "I need . . ."   "I want . . ."
  "Can I have . . . ?"   "Give me . . ."
  "Would you buy . . . ?" "I need money for..."
  "Everybody's wearing . . ." "Can I get . . . ?"

- Write a letter, write a poem, or draw a picture for a friend or relative who lives more than fifty miles away.
- Never use a gift or spend birthday (or other occasion) money until you have written a thank-you note.
- Once a week do a chore around home without being asked. (Something you aren't usually required to do.)
- Smile at yourself in the mirror once a day.
- Give an anonymous gift to someone who needs one. (No fair to let that person find out it's from you.)

10
As Others See You

Most people have a really weird view of an only child.

> An only child has expensive chocolate candy for breakfast every morning.
> An only child has an ice-cream freezer and a soda pop dispenser handy in the bedroom.
> An only child in a department store may buy anything the heart desires.
> An only child has the right to stay up as late as he or she wishes.

Most only children really don't have any of these things. Most only children are just plain kids.

Reasons for These Ideas

Have you ever heard the expression, "The grass is always greener on the other side of the fence"?

Very often this is how people look at others. They think if you are wearing a new sweater today that you wear a new sweater every day, and they would like to be an only child so they could wear a new

As Others See You

sweater every day (even if this is the only brand-new sweater you have ever owned). If you have a bedroom to yourself, they wish they had a bedroom to themselves. They don't stop to think of the disadvantages of being an only child.

Many times people who are unhappy are quick to place the blame on anything that is handy.

For example, if they were poor when they were young, they blame being from a large family.

If their parents gave them a lot of responsibility when they were a child, they blame having younger brothers and sisters.

They seldom stop to think that even as an only child, their family might have been poor. Or they don't realize that their parents might have given them a lot of responsibility even if they had been an only child.

There have been a lot of studies in the past few years to compare the oldest child in a family, the middle children, the youngest child, and the only child. Of course, these studies are very general. In other words, if they say, "An only child tends to be a quiet person," you could probably find exceptions. If you are quiet, you could probably find in your school a child with no brothers or sisters who is noisy. So the results of studies on brothers, sisters, and only children do not always apply to every person.

But when people have a weakness, they like to

point to a study and say, "See? It says that the middle child (the child with an older sibling and a younger sibling) tends not to plan so well. That's why I'm disorganized. It's because I'm a middle child."

The Way Friends See You

To some young people, whether or not they are only children makes no difference. To others, it makes a big difference.

It is possible not to have anyone know you're an only child. It is not something that makes you ugly or smell bad.

David never told anyone he was an only child. When friends came over to his house, they would ask where his brothers or sisters were, and he would say they were at his grandparents'. When asked where their room was, he would keep the upstairs bathroom door shut and say *that* was their room. Of course, lying never gets anyone anywhere, and he was eventually caught in his lie, but he was able to keep the truth a secret for some time.

Most people, the ones who are really worth your friendship, look at you as *you*.

> If you are nice . . .
> If you are easy to get along with . . .
> If you can do some things well but *not* everything . . .
> If you are not bossy . . .

If you like to laugh . . .

If you are a neat person . . .

They won't care what size your family is.

School

Because most only children are exposed to many adults and can get along well with them, they usually have few problems with teachers—unless they have a just plain troublesome teacher. Teachers and other school employees usually tend to like only children.

Another advantage of being an only is that parents can give more attention to your school studies. They can attend school activities, help with homework, and advise you on projects, while they wouldn't be able to give you as much of their time if you had brothers or sisters.

Envy

Anything one person has that another person does not have can be cause for envy. If Mr. Jones gets a new car and his neighbor Mr. Smith does not have a new car, Mr. Smith will almost certainly feel envious. Mr. Smith will wish *he* had a new car.

Let's say Jane wins a prize because she can dance very well, but Mary has never had dancing lessons. Mary cannot dance and does not win a prize, but Mary will almost certainly feel envious of Jane.

While Mr. Smith is grumbling and wishing he had a new car, he never stops to think about *how* Mr. Jones got the new car. Mr. Smith doesn't stop to think that while he was out bowling, Mr. Jones was working a night job to earn extra money. Nor does Mr. Smith think of the disadvantages Mr. Jones will have in owning a new car: the taxes, the license, the maintenance, the gas, the dozen or more people who will phone to ask for a ride to the store in the new car.

Mary, too, never stops to think about what Jane did to deserve her prize. Mary never considers the many hours of lessons Jane attended while Mary was home watching television. Mary never realizes that while she was playing, Jane was practicing her dancing.

Many people probably envy an only child. They might not say anything, but they are envious nevertheless. They might envy the things only children have or the opportunities they seem to enjoy, like lessons or places they get to go.

What Should You Say?

There are a few weird people in the world who might say something that will show they are jealous, like, "Oh, you might know he would have one of those. After all, he *is* an only child."

Or they might say something to show they feel sorry, like, "It's no wonder you don't know that. After all, you're an only child."

At times like these, it would be nice to reply with

a smart remark, something that would really put such people in their place.

Actually, it is best to say nothing. Probably arguing all day would never change their mind. In fact, arguing would probably just further convince them they are right about only children.

The best response is to smile and agree with them. This will not only surprise them, but maybe even make them a little sorry they said what they did.

If you are an okay kid, nice, polite, and good-natured, people with the unkind remarks will soon forget why they felt the way they did. Soon they'll just enjoy being around you. And you'll have the satisfaction of having really *changed* their mind!

11
Minuses in Being an Only

Unfortunately, this world isn't perfect, no human being is perfect, and life as an only child won't be perfect either. Here are some disadvantages in not having brothers or sisters to grow up with.

Parents

Parents of an only child tend to worry more about the child.

Parents of an only child tend to be more protective of the child.

If a parent had a dream or an ambition that never came true, he or she might want the child to complete that dream. In other words, if a father always wanted to be a lawyer but was never able to become one, he might make that his dream for his child and push the only youngster he has into *his* dream.

Expectations

Some parents have high expectations for their children, and if there is only one child, that one gets all the pressure. For instance, some parents expect good school grades. Others expect excellence in sports or a cultural activity such as music or writing or art. It

Minuses in Being an Only 93

is not too much to ask that you do your best, but unfortunately that is not good enough for some parents. If you are really trying, but still have trouble meeting your parents' expectations, ask an adult friend or relative or teacher to try to talk with your mother or father, or both.

Discipline

In a family of eight children, if a bedroom is messy, the mother probably closes the door. In a family of one child, if a bedroom is messy, the mother scolds. It boils down to this: With a big family, parents have to overlook some things or end up yelling all the time. It gets easier with each child just to ignore some misbehavior. (And someone said only children are spoiled!)

When parents have a lot of children, they have experimented with various forms of discipline on the older ones. The only child gets all the experiments—and maybe some mistakes!

Brothers and Sisters

Brothers and sisters obviously make a family larger. And a large family is more interesting because of the different personalities. When everyone is on good terms, a big family can be more fun.

Brothers and sisters get a sense of identity from one another.

Some people say the lack of competition is a disadvantage. They say family competition stimulates people to succeed in the world. This, of course, can be debated, since Chapter 13 mentions some very famous people who were only children and succeeded in worldwide competition!

A brother or sister is usually some comfort if there is a death or divorce in a family. At least for a while, brothers and sisters tend to band together and support one another. However, the person with no brothers or sisters must turn to others for listening and advice.

Brothers and sisters often stick up for one another.
Brothers and sisters trade chores.
Brothers and sisters share belongings.

Personality

Too much time spent with adults is a disadvantage in some people's view.

Only children tend to be loners, and this is thought to be a disadvantage by some people.

12
Pluses in Being an Only

There are plenty of advantages in being an only child. You can probably add even more to this list.

Parents

You might say, "Oh, yeah, sure, there are lots of advantages for my parents." But when your parents are happy, they can make a better homelife for you.

When parents are pressured by several children, their patience sometimes wears thin. But with only one child, there is less stress, so they are generally better able to cope and have more patience.

When parents have more time, they can be more creative with their own talents. Does your mother or father cook, sew, do crafts, paint, or write? Do they garden, build model planes, or participate in sports? If your parents are creatively busy, it may be because they have only one child and can afford the time and the money.

More time and more freedom to be creative or to study makes parents more interesting—not only to the world but to the child as well.

Parents with only one child have more time for

their own marriage. A couple has to have time to talk, to keep up common interests. A husband and wife with a lot of children seldom have time to devote to the marriage itself. A better marriage means a happier homelife.

By having only one child, a mother can more easily choose to go out to work or stay home. With more children, she might be forced into a decision she didn't want. For example, she might be forced to go get a job in order to have more money to pay the expenses of many children. Or she might be forced to stay home when she really wanted to return to her career simply because there was too much work to do or because day care for the children cost too much.

Family closeness is another advantage of being an only child. Only children have a closer relationship with their parents. When they have problems to discuss, their privacy time is not so limited. With brothers and sisters, a child might never get a chance to talk problems out with a parent. But an only child has plenty of opportunities.

If the parents really don't want more children, a sister or brother could be an "unwanted" child and might suffer.

Households with only one child are often more democratic than homes where there are many children. For example, "Should our new car be red or green?" is a decision in which an only child might have a voice. In a large family, however, it might be solely the parents' decision.

Fun Advantages

There are many things an only child is more likely to have or be exposed to than a child from a family with brothers and sisters: lessons (music, dance, gymnastic, swimming, etc.), cultural experiences (art, music, literature, museums, theater), trips and vacations, summer camp, entertainment, material possessions, visits to relatives, own bedroom, and privacy.

Brothers and Sisters

There are many advantages of having no brothers or sisters. Here are some examples:

- It is easier to grow up without having to compete for parents' attention.
- It is easier to grow up without competition from brothers or sisters.
- It is easier to grow up without having to compete for parents' time.
- It is easier to grow up without having to compete for parents' approval.
- It is easier to grow up without having to compete for parents' affection.
- It is easier to grow up without sibling rivalry.
- It is easier to grow up without comparisons to

brothers or sisters by parents and teachers.

It is easier to grow up without comparisons to brothers or sisters *by* the brothers or sisters.

It is easier to grow up without having your privacy invaded by brothers or sisters.

It is easier to grow up without having to be responsible for younger brothers or sisters.

It is easier to grow up without having to be responsible to older brothers or sisters.

A brother or sister might be smarter, more talented, more popular, more attractive, or more athletic than you.

An older brother might make you feel like a creep.

A younger sister might be a brat and a pest.

No parents ever intend to like one child better than another, but as one mother of two said, "Sometimes it's hard to love them equally when one is generous and helpful and always smiling and the other is always complaining or throwing things or making demands."

Wouldn't it be awful to do your best every day of your life, trying to make your parents like you, and yet feel they like another child best?

Or suppose you were the favorite. Perhaps you would feel:

- guilty, knowing you're not really any better than the others and not really deserving of better treatment
- cornered, knowing you always have to act or

talk or behave a certain way in order to keep the favored spot
- isolated, since the other brothers and sisters don't include you in their "less favored" family unit

Intelligence

Many, many studies have compared the intelligence of children raised with brothers or sisters against only children. These studies show that onlies are smarter!

Only children—and eldest children—usually have highest scores on intelligence tests and in their schoolwork. Only children are more often on the list of National Merit Scholars (a list of *smart* people!) than are those who have brothers and sisters.

Why?

All the advantages discussed in this chapter play a role. Generally, only children have more educational advantages, no sibling rivalry, and more of their parents' time.

And all this gives them a better chance to exercise their minds.

Personality

More time spent with adults is an advantage to a child.

Also, only children tend to be loners—people who prefer to be and do things alone.

You will find these two "advantages" on the "disadvantages" list in Chapter 11. There is no proof either way as to whether spending more time with adults is an advantage or a disadvantage. Some people say only children who don't have other children around never have a real childhood. This probably depends on the family more than on the fact that the child is an only.

"Only children tend to be loners" can go either way, as well. It is a disadvantage to be a loner if you make yourself into a hermit or a recluse, if you never reach out. But it is no crime to be a loner. A wise man once said, "Nine tenths of the people in this world were made so we would want to be with the other tenth." If he was right, is it really wrong to avoid the nine tenths we don't want to be with?

People who have studied personalities have discovered that only children tend to be superior in:

- intelligence
- independence
- courtesy
- honesty
- willingness to work
- ability to start a project or follow an interest
- self-control
- originality
- cooperation
- promptness
- carrying out promises
- health habits, including diet and exercise
- personal orderliness
- fantasy life
- obeying the law
- fairness
- generosity

13
Famous Only Children

Many famous people grew up as only children. They put together the advantages and disadvantages of their lone growing-up time and succeeded, partly *because* they were onlies.

Here are the names of a few in different fields. Reading magazines, newspapers, and biographies will turn up many more who can be role models for the only child growing up today.

Lauren Bacall and Carol Channing are famous only-child actresses. On the leading-man list are Robert DeNiro, Keir Dullea, and Al Pacino. Anthony Newley developed many talents and writes, composes, sings, and directs, as well as being an actor. Sammy Davis, Jr., entertainer, had a sister, but he was raised as an only child. Shirley Jones was an only, and so was Stanley Kramer, the producer and director. Famous stars of the past who grew up alone include Marilyn Monroe and Clark Gable.

Giant among artists of the past was Leonardo da Vinci, sculptor and scientist as well as painter. Today he is sometimes interpreted for us by only-child Kenneth Clark, art historian and teacher in university and on television. Rudi Gernreich, fashion designer, was also an only.

Alvin Ailey and Fernando Bujones are famous onlies in the field of the dance. The late black jazz musician Eubie Blake grew up alone, as did Burt Bacharach, Elton John, Buffy Sainte-Marie, Elvis Presley, and Frank Sinatra. Don McLean, singer, performer, and composer, had a sister, but she was fifteen years older, so that he felt he had "two mothers."

On the international political scene, Franklin D. Roosevelt, the thirty-second president, had only a half brother who was twenty-seven years older than he. Indira Gandhi is an only as well.

On Christmas Eve 1968 the first Apollo crew to reach the moon consisted of three astronauts. All three are only children: Frank Borman, James A. Lovell, Jr., and William A. Anders. Growing up alone must supply some of the inner resources helpful in outer space, because M. Scott Carpenter and L. Gordon Cooper are onlies too.

Thomas Alva Edison, the inventor, grew up alone and so did Charles Lindbergh, who first flew the Atlantic solo in 1927. Only sports greats include Joe Montana and Roger Staubach.

Onlies are good comedians, too, if Dick Cavett, Tim Conway, and Jonathan Winters are examples.

Growing up without siblings handy seems to nourish the kind of imagination a writer needs. Isabelle Holland's older brother was off to boarding school while she was growing up, and so was Beatrix Potter's. Many other famous authors, from Hans Christian Andersen of *Ugly Duckling* fame to Arthur Hailey, who wrote *Hotel,* were lone children. Columnist Erma Bombeck and author James Michener were also only children. Margaret Truman, only child of President Harry S. Truman, married only-child journalist Clifton Daniel and became a noted mystery writer.

An only child is a very special person, both growing up and grown-up.

Index

adoption, 19–20, 37–38, 64
advantages of onlies, 82–83, 87, 95–99
age, parents', 23, 29
Ailey, Alvin, 102
alone times, 60–72, 77–78
Anders, William A., 102
Andersen, Hans Christian, 102–103
anger, 55–56
appreciation, child's, 82
arguments
　between parents, 18–19
　with parents, 37
assumptions about onlies, 26–27, 86
attitudes toward onlies, 84, 88–89

baby-sitters, 14, 21, 22
Bacall, Lauren, 101
Bacharach, Burt, 102
Blake, Eubie, 102
Bombeck, Erma, 103
boredom, cure, 66–72
Borman, Frank, 102
bossiness, 43–44
brothers and sisters
　advantages to having, 40, 41, 93–94
　advantages to not having, 60–61, 97–99
　in real life, 61–62
　substitutes, 45, 64
Bujones, Fernando, 102

careers, parents', 20–21
Carpenter, M. Scott, 102
Cavett, Dick, 102
Channing, Carol, 101
chores
　children's, 73–74
　parents', 24
Clark, Kenneth, 101
clubs, 68, 75–76
Conway, Tim, 102
Cooper, L. Gordon, 102
cost of raising children, 14–16

cousins, 36
crafts, 67–69
creativity, 62

Daniel, Clifton, 103
Davis, Sammy, Jr., 101
death of parent, 33–35, 57, 94
definition of only child, 11–12
DeNiro, Robert, 101
difficult times, 31–35, 57, 75, 94
disadvantages to being an only, 92–94
discipline, 93
divorce, 19, 31–33, 94
Dullea, Keir, 101

Edison, Thomas Alva, 102
energy, parents', 17, 21
expectations, parents', 81–82, 92–93

family relationships, 30–41, 97
famous onlies, 101–103
fantasy world, 62–64
faults, parents', 37
feelings about being an only, 55–59
friends, 42–50
  adults, 51–52
  attitudes of, 84
  how to treat, 46–50
  loss of, 52
  new, 50–52, 75–76

Gable, Clark, 101
Gandhi, Indira, 102
Gernreich, Rudi, 101
gladness, 55–58
grandparents, 35–36

Hailey, Arthur, 103
health, parents', 19, 24
hobbies, 68
Holland, Isabelle, 102

imagination, 62–64
independence, 78–79
intelligence of onlies, 99

jealousy, 56, 89–90
jobs
  for children, 70–71
  of parents, 20–21, 56
John, Elton, 102
Jones, Shirley, 101

Kramer, Stanley, 101

Leonardo da Vinci, 101
Lindbergh, Charles, 102
loneliness, 57, 60–61
Lovell, James A., Jr., 102

Index

marriage problems, 18–19
material possessions, 82–83
McLean, Don, 102
meeting people, 53, 75–76
Michener, James, 103
money, 14–16, 47
   children earning, 70–72
Monroe, Marilyn, 101
Montana, Joe, 102

Newley, Anthony, 101
noise, 16

obligations, parents', 24–25, 81–82
older people as friends, 51–52
one-parent family, 18–19, 31–35, 73

Pacino, Al, 101
parents
   advantages to having an only, 95–97
   disadvantages to having an only, 39–40, 92–94
   friendship of, 50–51
   relationship to, 39–40

past, parents' family history, 22
patience, parents', 24
perfection
   in children, 25, 92–93
   in parents, 37
personality of onlies, 88, 94, 99–100
pets, 64
population explosion, 21
Potter, Beatrix, 102
Presley, Elvis, 102
priorities, parents', 17–18
privacy, 22, 61–62, 98
privileges, 80–85, 88

reasons a child is an only, 14–25, 28–29
responsibility, 80–84
Roosevelt, Franklin D., 102
rules for friendship, 45–50
rumors about onlies, 27

Sainte-Marie, Buffy, 102
school, 89
selfishness, 42–43
separation from parents, 76–77
shame, 57
sharing, 22, 42–43, 47–50
Sinatra, Frank, 102
spoiled children, 80–84

Staubach, Roger, 102
substitute brothers and sisters, 45, 64–66

television, 29, 65–66
things to do, 66–72, 75–76
time with parents, 16–17

tools of imagination (toys), 62
Truman, Margaret, 103

unspoiling, 84–85

volunteering, 33, 68

Winters, Jonathan, 102

About the Author

Charlotte Foltz Jones is married and lives with her husband and their son (and their cat) in Boulder, Colorado. She was born, raised, and educated in Boulder, at the foot of the Rocky Mountains.

The author has first-hand experience with the subject of the only child. Not only is she the mother of an only, but she, too, is an only child. She never enjoyed being an only, but her son loves it.

A former secretary in the public school system, Mrs. Jones devotes her time to freelance writing and homemaking. Her articles and stories have appeared in children's, teen, women's, and religious magazines as well as in business and general interest publications.

She attributes her writing ability to the genes but credits creative writing teachers Jane Fitz-Randolph and Barbara Steiner for honing her skills.

Knitting, crocheting, and sewing are her personal hobbies. Railroading and camping are family interests. Mrs. Jones and her husband also pride themselves in having entirely constructed the house in which they live.